W I

AUG '93
AUG '93
AUG '93

THE CENTRAL ASIAN STATES

TAJIKISTAN • UZBEKISTAN
KYRGYZSTAN • TURKMENISTAN

By
Paul Thomas

The Millbrook Press
Brookfield, Connecticut

©Aladdin Books Ltd 1992

Designed and produced by
Aladdin Books Ltd
28 Percy Street
London W1P 9FF

First published in the
United States in 1992 by
The Millbrook Press
2 Old New Milford Road
Brookfield, Connecticut 06804

The consultant is Dr. John Channon of the School of
Slavonic and Eastern European Studies, London, UK.

Series Design: David West
Designer: Rob Hillier
Editor: Catherine Bradley
Picture Research: Emma Krikler

Library of Congress Cataloging-in-Publication Data

Thomas, Paul. 1952-
    The Central Asian states/by Paul Thomas:
John Channon, consultant.
        p. cm -- (Former Soviet states)
    Includes bibliographical references and index.
    Summary: Describes the history, development,
current status, and possible future of the four former Soviet
republics which have strong ties to neighboring Muslim states.
    ISBN 1-56294-307-3 (lib. bdg.)
    1. Asia, Central--Juvenile literature. (1. Asia, Central.
2. Tajikistan. 3. Uzbekistan. 4. Kyrgyzstan.)
I. Title. II. Series.
DK851.T47 1992
958--dc20   92-2239 CIP AC

Printed in Belgium

CONTENTS

INTRODUCTION

Turkmenistan, Uzbekistan, Tajikistan, and Kyrgyzstan have rarely been at the center of world events. They lie at the heart of the Eurasian landmass. Before the discovery of oil and natural gas in the twentieth century, the area was noted for its undeveloped lifestyle. The people lived a nomadic existence, tending herds of sheep, goats, and horses. In the very distant past the southern cities of Bukhara and Samarkand were famous for their wealth, based on trade. In the nineteenth century the area came under the control of the Russian Empire. When the communists took over, the central Asian states endured great hardships as well as some economic and other benefits. Today Uzbekistan, Turkmenistan, Tajikistan, and Kyrgyzstan are members of the Commonwealth of Independent States (C.I.S.), which was established in December 1991. They face grave difficulties in coping with their new-found independence.

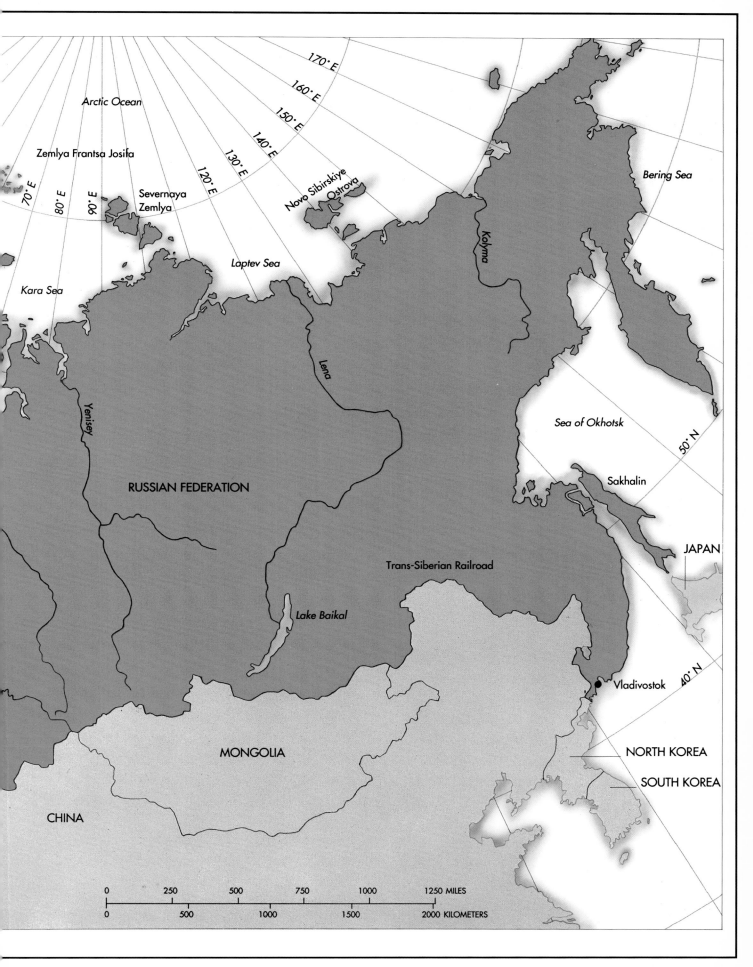

Arctic Ocean

Zemlya Frantsa Josifa

170° E

160° E

150° E

140° E

130° E

120° E

Bering Sea

70° E

80° E

90° E

Severnaya
Zemlya

Novo Sibirskiye
Ostrova

Kolyma

Laptev Sea

Kara Sea

Lena

Yenisey

Sea of Okhotsk

50° N

RUSSIAN FEDERATION

Sakhalin

JAPAN

Trans-Siberian Railroad

Lake Baikal

40° N

Vladivostok

MONGOLIA

NORTH KOREA

SOUTH KOREA

CHINA

| 0 | 250 | 500 | 750 | 1000 | 1250 MILES |

| 0 | 500 | 1000 | 1500 | 2000 KILOMETERS |

THE STATES TODAY

A prayer meeting in a mosque in Tashkent, September 1990

The newly independent Uzbekistan, Turkmenistan, Tajikistan, and Kyrgyzstan are members of the C.I.S., which replaced the Soviet Union. After seven years of trying to reform the Soviet Union's economy, it was clear that the union could no longer be held together. Eleven of the former Soviet republics decided to go for independence within a commonwealth, to resolve any outstanding problems.

The four central Asian states are also members of the United Nations, and are developing both diplomatic and trade links with neighboring countries and the international community. Turkey, Iran, Pakistan, and Saudi Arabia all show a serious interest in developing the backward economies of the central Asian states. The natural resources of Turkmenistan and Uzbekistan, in particular, natural gas, oil, and suitable growing conditions for cotton, make them attractive to foreign investors. The economic potential of an area with over 35 million inhabitants has encouraged Japan and South Korea to send trade missions to the region.

Together the four central Asian states have one of the largest Muslim populations in the world, over 25-30 million; the number of mosques in the area has risen from 150 to 5,000 since 1989. The peoples of the four states are Sunni Muslims, following the sect of Islam favored by Saudi Arabia, Turkey, and Afghanistan, and it is inevitable that links with these countries will increase. The growth of support for the Islamic Renaissance Party, which favors the creation of Muslim states similar to Iran, has been viewed with alarm by the ruling groups in the central Asian states.

The Uzbek, Turkmen, and Kyrgyz

peoples all speak a Turkic language, and as a result have close ties with Turkey. Tajikistan is the only central Asian state whose language is not of Turkic origin; the Tajiks speak Farsi, the language spoken by the Iranians. Closer relations between the two nations appear likely, although the fact that Iran practices the minority Shi'ite sect of Islam may limit its influence. Turkmenistan shares a common border with Iran, and plans for economic cooperation in oil refining are well advanced.

The states include a great mixture of peoples. There are substantial numbers of Uzbeks living in Tajikistan, and Tajiks in Kyrgyzstan. In the 1980s and early 1990s there were clashes between rival groups and it is likely that adjustments to the borders of the states may be the only solution to this ethnic problem. In February 1990, there were riots in Tajikistan following rumors that Armenians were to settle in the country. In June 1989, Uzbeks attacked Meskhetians in Uzbekistan. The Meskhetians had been forcibly deported to the area in 1944, and were never allowed to return to their homes in Georgia. Some 100 Meskhetians died and over 16,000 of them were deported to the Russian Federation. In June 1990,

A gas-processing plant, Uzbekistan

An injured Meskhetian, June 1989

there was fighting between Uzbeks and Kyrgyz in Kyrgyzstan and 148 people were reported to have died. Many of the Russians who have lived in the area since the 1920s have left since independence, perhaps fearing an Islamic revolution, but also worried about their economic future.

The problems facing the states are considerable; for decades the poorest republics in the Soviet Union, they relied heavily on the Russian republic to buy their natural resources in exchange for manufactured goods and subsidized, cheap food. The states could have grown their own food, but under the Soviet system were forced to produce crops, such as cotton, jute, and tobacco, which could be sold abroad. The need to produce these non-food crops has created an ecological disaster in the Aral Sea area, which needs to be solved jointly by the central Asian states.

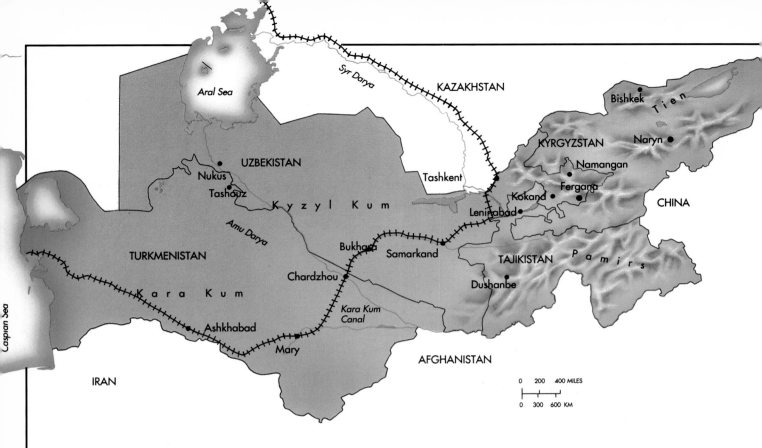

PEOPLE AND PLACES

The region borders two major inland seas, the Aral and the Caspian. Into the Aral Sea flow the two most important rivers of central Asia, the Amu Darya and Syr Darya, formerly known as the Oxus and the Jaxartes. These two rivers originate in the Pamir and Tien Shan mountain ranges, which are over 24,000 feet (7,315 meters) high, and covered in snow all year round. The world's fourth largest desert lies in this area of central Asia, the Kara Kum, so-called because of its black sand. To the southeast of the Aral Sea lies another large desert, the Kyzyl Kum, meaning red sand.

Uzbekistan is varied and colorful, with the vast Tien Shan and Pamir mountain ranges in the south, and the Kyzyl Kum desert in the northeast. The northwest of the country is bordered by the Aral Sea,

and it is here that cotton is grown. Uzbekistan is the largest cotton-producing area in the commonwealth, and has deposits of both oil and natural gas sufficient for its own domestic needs.

The black sands of Kara Kum

The Tashkent metro built with Soviet money

Gold mining and chemical industries are of importance to the economy, as are tobacco and grain. At just over 20 million, the population of Uzbekistan is the third largest in the C.I.S., and is growing rapidly. Tashkent, the capital, is the fourth largest city in the C.I.S., with over two million inhabitants.

Turkmenistan lies to the east of the Caspian Sea, sharing borders with Afghanistan and Iran to the south, and Uzbekistan and Kazakhstan to the north. More than 80 percent of the state is desert – the Kara Kum. Large reserves of natural gas are Turkmenistan's main natural asset, and it supplies 11 percent of the total production of the C.I.S. Substantial deposits of oil may also be present beneath the Kara Kum. The state has just over 3.7 million people.

Tajikistan is the most southerly of the central Asian states. Lying to the west of China, it shares a common border with Afghanistan, Uzbekistan, and Kyrgyzstan. Most of the country consists of high mountain ranges, the Pamirs. The western part of Tajikistan slopes down to the plains of central Asia, where there is farming. Cotton is grown, but not on the same scale as in Uzbekistan. There are few natural resources in Tajikistan apart from hydroelectric power and some mining of lead and bauxite. It is hoped that there are oil deposits in the western part of the country. It has a population of approximately five million. The Tajiks have traditionally led a nomadic life, and there are substantial numbers of Tajiks living outside the borders of the country in both Uzbekistan and Afghanistan.

Kyrgyzstan is a mountainous country sharing borders with Kazakhstan in the north, Tajikistan to the south, Uzbekistan in the west, and China to the east. It has a population of some four million which is made up of many different peoples. Only half the population is native Kyrgyz. There are substantial numbers of European Russians, Muslim Tajiks, Volga Germans, and Asiatic Uighurs, five million of whom live in neighboring China. Kyrgyzstan relies heavily on livestock farming, and for centuries the nomadic Kyrgyz have tended their flocks on the Tien Shan mountain pastures. More recently the country has harnessed the power of the many mountain rivers.

A traditional nomad tent, a yurta, in Kyrgyzstan

THE EARLY HISTORY OF THE REGION

The earliest evidence of human activity in the area goes back to about 40,000 B.C. The remains of classical Neanderthal man were discovered at Teshik-Tash in the mountains to the southeast of the central Asian states. The high mountains and harsh climate of the region made it uninviting to the early peoples of Asia, but nomadic peoples have lived there for nearly four thousand years.

For centuries waves of people traveled across the grasslands or steppes of central Asia in search of good grazing for their animals. People moved mainly from east to west, from deepest Asia. This was because of the rise in the number of people there. Languages also spread westward with the people. The Aryans who invaded northern India in about 1500 B.C. are thought to have come from an area between the Caspian and Aral seas.

The Silk Road

The first towns in the area were along the Silk Road, one of the world's oldest roads, linking China with central Asia, the Middle East, and the Mediterranean Sea.

The city of Samarkand, in present-day Uzbekistan, dates back to 2,000 B.C. and was an important center on the route. The region was at the crossroads of the route from India, and

The early settlers measured their wealth in terms of the number of sheep and camels they owned.

A Samarkand dome

merchants employed caravans of camels to exchange silk from China, cotton from India, jade from central Asia, and glass from the West.

Wheels and horses

Ideas, inventions, and religions also traveled along the Silk Road in ancient times, enriching the areas through which they passed.

Some archaeologists believe that the wheel may have been developed in central Asia. What is certain is that a particularly strong breed of horse originated there, from which the modern Arabian horses are descended.

The fame of the horses bred in the Fergana Valley attracted the attention of the Chinese Emperor Wu in the second century B.C. He sent an ambassador to what is now Uzbekistan and Kyrgyzstan: his report confirmed the quality of the horses and described a fertile land with prosperous fields, as well as some 70 walled cities. The emperor dispatched an army "many tens of thousands strong" to obtain stocks of the "heavenly horses," as a Chinese hymn of the first century B.C. described them, but this ambitious expedition never reached Fergana.

Central Asian foothills have long been home to wild horses.

AT THE CROSSROADS OF EMPIRES

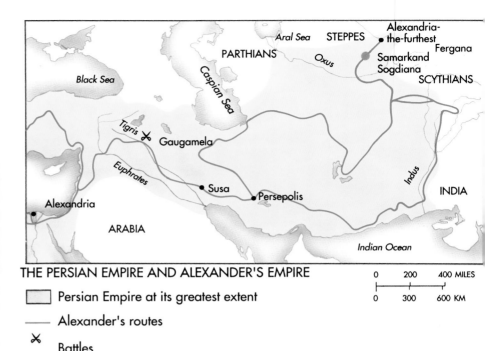

THE PERSIAN EMPIRE AND ALEXANDER'S EMPIRE

☐ Persian Empire at its greatest extent

— Alexander's routes

✕ Battles

| 0 | 200 | 400 MILES |
| 0 | 300 | 600 KM |

The Silk Road explains why this part of central Asia has such a vivid and violent history, attracting the attention of empire builders keen to conquer new lands. One of the first empires to unite the vast area between the Indus and the Mediterranean Sea was the Persian Empire. This stretched as far north as the Oxus River, almost to the Aral Sea, and dominated central and western Asia from the sixth century B.C. Its capital was at Persepolis in southern Iran.

The Persian Empire

The empire was efficient, with a system of laws, roads, postal services, and a tradition of religious toleration. It was divided into 20 satrapies, or administrative units, each of which paid taxes to Persepolis.

For two centuries Persian rule ensured peace and stability on the western Asian section of the Silk Road, and brought prosperity to trading centers such as Maracanda, later Samarkand, the capital of the Sogdiana satrapy.

Agriculture improved through better irrigation methods. This led to the spread of fruit growing, of particular importance in the Oxus Valley, as well as the cultivation of alfalfa, which was a fodder crop for horses.

The Persians left their mark on central Asia in the form of buildings and their civilization. However, their empire eventually fell to an invader who came from the west, rather than the east.

The Hellenistic Empire

Alexander the Great aimed to avenge the attacks Persia had launched on Greece in the fifth century B.C. He managed to carve out one of the greatest empires of all times, which was to stretch all the way from Greece to northern India.

Alexander the Great

Crossing to Asia in 334 B.C., Alexander routed the Persians at the battle of Gaugamela in 331 B.C., and during the eight years before his death established an empire that covered two million square miles (5,180,000 sq. km). Alexander found it difficult to overcome the Sogdian armies and to cross the Oxus and Jaxartes rivers.

He spent time in Samarkand and Tashkent, and established a new city to control the region; it was named Alexandria-the-furthest, later to become Khojend. The city was to be a base against the Scythians, a warlike people from northern Asia, who threatened Alexander's northwestern border.

Under pressure

Within 50 years of Alexander's death his empire had disintegrated into separate kingdoms. However, the many Greek cities and colonies that Alexander left behind gave the peoples of central Asia civilization and some military organization. For several centuries they were able to withstand the Scythians and the Parthians, another nomadic people pressing southward from the steppes.

Other threats

From the east in the second century B.C. came the Chinese in search of horses from the Fergana Valley. Meanwhile, from India, the Kushan empire was expanding its influence westward through trade.

The Kushans used a 2,600-mile (4,200-km) Grand Road, which joined up with the Silk Road at Bactra, a city in Afghanistan, close to the Oxus River. In Iran the Sasanian Empire also developed trade and had much influence over central Asia from the third to the seventh centuries A.D., but had little lasting effect on the region.

During this time the peoples of central Asia faced constant pressure from nomadic peoples. The Huns and the Avars, forced to search for water and goods as the steppes became increasingly dry, raided the southern cities of Bukhara and Samarkand.

A heavily laden caravan crosses the central Asian desert.

RELIGION AND THE SPREAD OF ISLAM

Religion became of crucial importance in central Asia from about the time of the birth of Christ. For many centuries the area had been subject to the influence of various religions, which spread along the Silk Road.

Buddhism
The Buddhist faith started in India in the sixth century B.C. Buddhist missionaries traveled along the Silk Road in the latter part of the first century B.C. They spread their beliefs and made converts.

Zoroastrianism
Another religion was Zoroastrianism, named after its founder, Zoroaster, which began at about the same time as Buddhism. It spread through Asia and became the official religion of the Sasanian Dynasty.

This dynasty revived the glories of past Persian empires by driving the Buddhists out of central

A mosque built in the ancient city of Bukhara

Asia in the third century A.D. It also took control of Samarkand, Tashkent, and the silk trade. The farthest limit of the Sasanian Empire was the Pamir mountain range in the east and the Oxus River to the north, an area the dynasty controlled until the beginning of the seventh century.

Christianity
Christianity arrived in central Asia around the fourth and fifth centuries,

having spread from the Middle East, from cities at the western end of the Silk Road, such as Antioch and Tarsus. Christians built many churches in Samarkand and Bukhara.

The spread of Islam
These were the competing religions in central Asia when the death of the Arabian prophet, Muhammad, in 632 led to the spread of Islam. Muslim armies carried the new faith from Arabia into

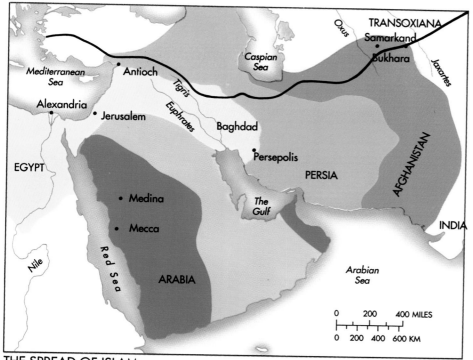

THE SPREAD OF ISLAM

- Islamic Empire under Muhammad
- Islamic expansion 632 – 634
- Islamic expansion 634 – 661
- Expansion under Umayyad Caliphs (661 – 750)
- Expansion under Abbasid Caliphs (750 – 850)
— The Silk Road

Asia, Africa, and Europe, creating an empire larger than Alexander's.

The Persians were overrun within decades of the prophet's death, as was much of North Africa and the Near East. Samarkand, Bukhara, and other cities of Transoxiana, as the region was then known, fell to the Muslim armies in 710.

At first the Muslim conquerors allowed other religious groups, as Muhammad himself had done, but after 750 the Abbasid Caliphs demanded that their subjects convert to Islam.

They created a prosperous, well-run empire which made a great contribution to architecture, science, and literature. In the following centuries many of the peoples of central Asia became Muslim, as they are to this day. They followed the Sunni tradition.

Islam
The prophet Muhammad was born in Arabia about 570. He believed he was God's messenger and taught a new religion, Islam. His messages were written down in a book called the Koran. Islamic followers, known as Muslims, believe there is only one God, called Allah. After Muhammad's death, there was a dispute among his followers about who should lead the Muslims. The Sunnis followed the Caliphs, while the Shi'ites decided to follow Muhammad's cousin, Ali.

The prophet Muhammad

TRADE, TURKS, AND THE MONGOLS

Islam united a vast area of western Asia in religion and culture at the beginning of the tenth century. Pilgrims traveled west along the Silk Road to visit the sacred city of Mecca, Muhammad's birthplace. Many Muslims learned Arabic so they could study the Koran.

However, the Abbasid Caliphs lost control of their empire, which split into separate states but remained Muslim. One of these states was set up by a people called the Samanids, and it was centered in Bukhara and Samarkand.

Turkestan

Then the Seljuk Turks, nomads from the steppes of northeastern Asia, swept through Transoxiana in 1040, and conquered the lands which had made up the Abbasid Empire. They

In the early years of Islam trade prospered on the Silk Road. Silk was made in central Asia, and Muslim merchants traded with Arabia, the Byzantine Empire, and India, controlling the passage of spices, such as cloves and pepper from the Far East, as well as traditional goods like gold, jade, and silk.

became followers of Islam and established their capital at Baghdad. They also fought a series of holy wars in Palestine against Crusaders from Christian Europe.

They controlled land as far west as the country which still retains their name, Turkey. The lands of central Asia became known as Turkestan.

By the end of the twelfth century the Seljuks could no longer maintain their grip on Turkestan, and the Khwarezm took control of Samarkand and Bukhara. However,

This twelfth-century mausoleum was built in honor of a sultan at Mary in Turkmenistan.

soon they too faced a formidable enemy.

The Mongol Empire

The Mongolian tribes had been a simple nomadic people, living with their horses and herds on the steppes to the north of China until 1196. By that year Temujin, later to be known as Genghis Khan, had succeeded in uniting the Mongol people and at the age of 34 embarked on a military adventure that saw the creation of the largest empire Asia had ever known.

Turning first on China, the Mongols pierced the Great Wall, which had protected the Chinese from raiding warriors. The Mongols captured Beijing and occupied the northern half of the country.

Turning westward in 1219, Genghis Khan launched a ferocious attack on Turkestan at the head of a 200,000-strong army. Employing siege engineers captured in the Chinese campaigns, the Mongols overwhelmed Bukhara, Samarkand, and the other walled cities of the region, slaughtering tens of thousands of inhabitants. Only craftsmen whose skills

During the days of the Mongol Empire, European explorers and merchants began to travel farther into Asia. The Polo brothers visited Bukhara in 1265 on the way to China, while a decade later Marco Polo explored the Pamir Mountains in present-day Tajikistan.

the Mongols could use were spared in these massacres.

This terrible cruelty was supposed to frighten the peoples of central Asia and ensure their acceptance of Mongol rule. Genghis Khan swept on westward through Persia and the Caucasus into the modern-day Russian Federation.

Genghis Khan's death in 1227 only briefly interrupted the Mongol conquests, since his sons and grandsons carried on into Eastern Europe over the next century.

After the killing and looting had stopped, the Mongols brought a period of peace and prosperity to central Asia. They converted to Islam in the fourteenth century and the devastated cities of

Turkestan were rebuilt. Trade along the Silk Road increased because the Mongols developed an efficient communications network. This period became known as the Mongolian Peace, and European explorers and merchants began to travel deeper into Asia.

Genghis Khan

Tamerlane built many magnificent monuments in Samarkand.

SQUEEZED BETWEEN RIVALS

The rise of Russia

The Mongol armies devastated Russia, sacking Kiev in 1240 and destroying the main Russian cities. However, Mongol power declined in Russia during the next two hundred years. In the late fifteenth century the Russian princes made the most of this, and finally won their independence from the Mongols.

Ivan the Great, the first tsar, began to consolidate his lands, which by 1533 reached to the Caspian Sea and the Ural Mountains. The Russians expanded further eastward into Siberia, and by 1647, the Russian Empire stretched to the Pacific Ocean.

Mongol decline

After two centuries of power, Mongol rule in central Asia also began to decline. The last khan of any real importance was Tamerlane, whose dazzling empire was based at Samarkand, controlling the Silk Road. The region then disintegrated into numerous rival Muslim khanates, such as Khiva, Kokand, and Bukhara, which fought among themselves.

Russian conquest

It was not until the nineteenth century that the Russians tried to expand to Turkestan. The region was too remote, dangerous, and uncivilized. However, by this time Imperial Russia feared British expansion in the area.

The British Empire was the leading world power. The British wanted to make sure that the Russians did not threaten Afghanistan and their empire in India. A war of nerves developed as each side probed the other's strengths and weaknesses, employing spies and secret strategy to gain influence among the Muslim rulers of Central Asia.

Eventually Russia decided that it could not allow Turkestan to fall into British hands. The

British had just dealt with a serious rebellion in India when, in 1864, the invasion of Turkestan was launched, to free Russian citizens held captive as slaves in Khiva, or so it was claimed.

Tashkent, the richest city in central Asia, was taken in 1865, Samarkand in 1868, and Khiva in 1873. The invasion was to be permanent. The construction of the Trans-Caspian railroad began in 1880, linking the future capitals of Turkmenistan and Uzbekistan by the end of the decade.

The castle of Gissar in Tajikistan was built to protect a pass.

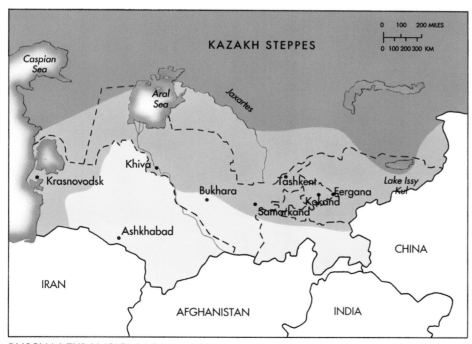

RUSSIAN EXPANSION 1856 – 1888

- Russian Empire 1856
- Acquired 1856 – 1868
- Acquired 1868 – 1888
- - - - Boundaries of the states today

Khivan cruelty

In the year 1717, some 4,000 Russian soldiers commanded by Count Bekovich arrived in Khiva, to be welcomed by the Muslim khan. The Russian soldiers were given places to stay in the city, but were then massacred as they slept. Count Bekovich's head was displayed on the city wall. Fewer than forty Russians managed to return from the ill-fated expedition. Turkestan and its cruel khans became notorious among Europeans after this bloody episode.

REVOLUTION AND WAR

By the early twentieth century the Russian Empire was in real difficulty. Its borders were overstretched, its peasants faced terrible hardships, and the Russian tsar, Nicholas II, was incompetent. In 1861 Alexander II had tried to help the peasants by giving them their freedom and a bit of land, but the vast majority were still desperately poor. Russia lost a war against Japan in 1905. After great unrest and a revolution, Nicholas agreed to allow an elected parliament, the Duma. This gave the Russian people a rare, if brief, experience of limited democracy.

The Russian Revolution

In 1914 Russia joined Britain and France in the war against Germany and Austria-Hungary, which became known as World War I. The war put an enormous strain on the Russian people and economy, provoking strikes, riots, and mutinies among soldiers and sailors. The tsarist system collapsed in February 1917. In central Asia the Russians had tried to conscript men to go to war. This had been very unpopular, and Tashkent became a center of Bolshevik (later known as communist) opposition to both the tsar and the provisional government that succeeded him. In September 1917, Tashkent became the first city to overthrow the local authorities of the provisional government. The following month the Bolshevik Party, led by Vladimir Lenin, seized power in Petrograd.

The Soviet Union

The Bolsheviks, or Reds as they were called, had to fight a civil war for

In the early twentieth century most of the inhabitants of Kyrgyzstan lived in great poverty.

This meeting took place to mark the founding of an Uzbek people's republic.

control of Russia against the Whites, anti-Bolsheviks who were helped by the country's former Allies in World War I. The Tashkent Bolsheviks did much to maintain Red control in central Asia, despite being cut off from Moscow by White armies for almost two years. By 1921 the Bolsheviks had gained their victory and they began to reorganize their lands, which officially became the Soviet Union in 1922. Industry, finance, and land were all brought under state control, enforced by a growing secret police.

Lenin died in 1924. Joseph Stalin took over and imposed new policies. The problem of clashes between different ethnic groups within the Soviet Union was addressed by creating separate Soviet republics. In 1925 the Uzbek, Tajik, and Turkmen Soviet Socialist Republics were established, while Kyrgyzia was included in Tajikistan until it also became a republic in 1936. The republics had little real power as Stalin imposed a brutal, centralized system.

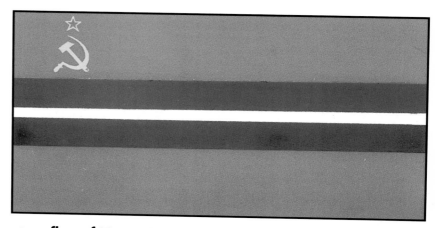

The state flag of Kyrgyzia, as Kyrgyzstan used to be known

THE SOVIET SYSTEM

Stalin's first aim after he became the leader of the Soviet Union was to develop the economy, which had been in ruins following the revolution and the civil war. He issued Five Year Plans which specified how much factories, mines, and other industries were to produce. All farms were brought under state control and collectivized between 1928 and 1932. This had a devastating effect on the central Asian states. The Uzbeks were forced to grow cotton, while nomads had to abandon the way of life they had followed for centuries. Not surprisingly, these policies led to famines between 1932 and 1934. It was not until the 1950s that the livestock farming recovered.

The purges
Stalin used collectivization to destroy the clan loyalties of the central Asian peoples, whose lives had not been greatly affected by communism. Stalin also tried to undermine Muslim influence by replacing the Arabic alphabet with a Latin version. In the late 1930s Stalin decided to purge the Communist Party and punish those who were "responsible" for the failure of his Five Year Plans. Millions of communists died throughout the Soviet Union.

Little progress
Stalin's rule saw the building of a few railroads and canals in central Asia and the creation of some new industries in the area. However, on the whole the economy of the region was disrupted and its people were terrorized. In 1941 the Soviet Union was invaded by Germany, and it fought in World War II alongside the United States, Great Britain, France, and other countries. The war did not affect the central Asian states directly, although serving in the army was deeply unpopular. Stalin's death in 1953 was mourned by few in central Asia.

Stagnation
Stalin's successor, Nikita Khrushchev, denounced Stalin for his brutality, but the inflexible, centralized system he had

Poster commemorating the Uzbek and Turkmen republics

Massoud (center) led the Mujahedeen fighters in Afghanistan.

established proved difficult to reform. In the central Asian states, power was in the hands of local communist leaders, whose power often came from the clans which they led.

Under Leonid Brezhnev, who succeeded Khrushchev in 1964, the Soviet system stagnated, with widespread corruption and inefficiency. International tension relaxed after the chilliness of the Cold War in the 1950s, but the invasion of Afghanistan in 1979 revived fears that the Soviet Union might want to expand. There was much disquiet among Muslims in Tajikistan as Soviet troops fought their Tajik relatives in Afghanistan, many of whom were Mujahedeen – Muslim freedom fighters.

Brezhnev died in 1982.

His death set the scene for the final years of the Soviet Union.

The breakup of the Soviet Union

Mikhail Gorbachev came to power in 1985. He promised to reform the Soviet system, and introduced *glasnost* (openness) and *perestroika* (restructuring). His reforms won him praise from the United States and Europe, but the problems of the Soviet Union were so difficult to sort out that the communist system collapsed.

Gorbachev survived a coup attempt in August 1991, but only with the help of Boris Yeltsin, the president of the Russian republic. Real power passed to Yeltsin in December 1991 with the creation of the Commonwealth of Independent States (C.I.S.) The Soviet Union no longer existed.

These apartments in Tashkent were built with Soviet subsidies.

OUTLOOK FOR UZBEKISTAN AND TURKMENISTAN

The present leader of Uzbekistan, President Islam Karimov, was elected in December 1991. A former communist leader, he now heads the People's Democratic Party of Uzbekistan, which has inherited all its staff and property from the old Communist Party. Uzbekistan has a tradition of political repression, police brutality, and corruption. Karimov recently pardoned a group of officials, jailed for corruption. They had exaggerated cotton production figures and received money from Moscow. Karimov does not allow other parties and has banned the Islamic Renaissance Party and the Birlick, or Unity Party. There is little prospect of democracy in Uzbekistan.

The language spoken in Uzbekistan is Turkic in origin, and Uzbekistan is developing trading links with Turkey. The success of Islamic groups in Tajikistan, with whom Uzbekistan has a border dispute, may mean that Uzbekistan will draw closer to Turkey and the more moderate Arab states of the Middle East, such as Saudi Arabia.

As one of the most modern central Asian states, and most rich in resources, Uzbekistan looks well-placed to develop economically. It has a large Korean community living within its borders, and has trade links with both China and Korea. However, the lack of political freedom and democracy may create tension and conflict, particularly with the Muslim people of the Fergana Valley in the east of the country.

The Aral Sea disaster

Uzbekistan and its neighbors face a major ecological disaster in the Aral Sea. This was once the fourth largest inland body of water in the world, fed by the Amu Darya and Syr Darya rivers. However, over the past 20 years the sea has shrunk by one third, because so much water has been diverted from the rivers for irrigation to grow cotton. The Aral has shrunk so much that Aralsk, in the past the main seaport, is now 60 miles from the shore. Now Uzbekistan must pay the price for overirrigation. Much of the irrigated land is salting up, as dust from the dry beds blows over it.

The countries of central Asia must agree to reduce their demands for water. However, they also need to develop economically. It will be difficult for the central Asian states to decide which is more important.

The Aral Sea left these fishing boats stranded.

Turkmenistan

President Saparmurad Niyazov, the former leader of the Communist Party, which is now known as the Democratic Party, retained power. No opposition parties have been allowed to operate, and there are no plans for political or economic reforms.

Turkmenistan is badly placed to cope with independence, since it grows little food, and the loss of subsidized supplies from the former Soviet Union will be felt deeply. However, the country produces 111 billion cubic yards (85 billion cubic meters) of natural gas per year from beneath the Kara Kum, of which 14 billion cubic yards (11 billion cubic meters) are destined for export in 1992. Turkmenistan supplies gas to Tajikistan, Uzbekistan, Kyrgyzstan, Iran, and other states within the C.I.S.

A new road is being built between the Iranian capital, Teheran, and Ashkhabad, the Turkmen capital. Turkey is improving television and telephone

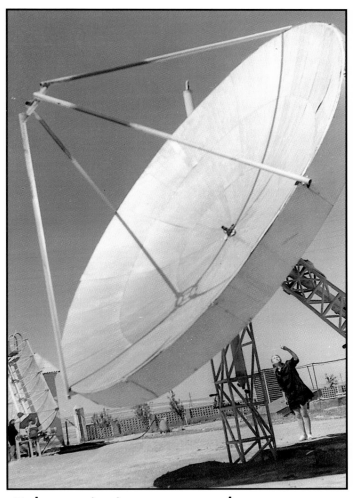

Turkmen scientists try to use solar power.

The capital of Turkmenistan, Ashkhabad

links using an Intelsat satellite, which the Turks have launched to unite the Turkish-speaking countries of central Asia. It is likely that a firm relationship will develop with Turkey, although trade with Iran is also important.

Muslim groups, however, present a problem for President Niyazov. The Islamic Renaissance Party held its founding congress in Ashkhabad in 1990, and it enjoys popular support among ordinary Turkmens. The lack of political freedom and the examples of Tajikistan and Afghanistan, where communist regimes have fallen to Islam, mean that Niyazov may not last long as president of Turkmenistan.

These soldiers fought to depose President Nabiev of Tajikistan in May 1992.

OUTLOOK FOR TAJIKISTAN AND KYRGYZSTAN

Tajikistan is one of the poorest and most politically volatile states of the Commonwealth. It was ruled by President Rakkhman Nabiev from November 1991 until May 1992. A former communist, he had dominated Tajik politics for 20 years. However, many Tajiks found they were worse off following the loss of cheap food and subsidized goods from the former Soviet Union. By April 1992 opposition to Nabiev had reached such a pitch that tens of thousands of Tajiks demonstrated in the capital, Dushanbe. In early May violence erupted, and after a three-day battle that left 70 Tajiks dead, Nabiev was overthrown.

There remains a distinct possibility of civil war since support for Nabiev's regime was very much clan-based, in the areas around Kulyab and Khodjeni. The Islamic Renaissance Party, which got 34 percent of the vote in the last election, draws its support from the east of the country. It is possible that Tajik members of the Afghan Mujahedeen, who overthrew the Afghan communists in 1992, could supply weapons to their Muslim brothers in Tajikistan.

Since becoming independent, Tajikistan has made little progress toward changing its economy. Although trade deals have been struck with Iran and Pakistan, it will take years for the country to develop. It can expect help from Saudi Arabia, which recently distributed a million free copies of the Koran among the central Asian states.

Kyrgyzstan

Despite clashes between rival ethnic groups in the 1980s and early 1990s, Kyrgyzstan is more stable than the other central Asian states. The credit for this must go to President Askar Akayez, who is a physicist and has never played a leading role in the Kyrgyz Communist Party. He was reelected in October 1991 unopposed, and has followed a policy of trying to bring his people together. His aim is to increase the prosperity of the country and create stability.

Before independence, Kyrgyzstan depended on the more developed parts

Saudi Arabian visitors in central Asia

of the Soviet Union for subsidized, cheap food and manufactured goods. It also has a sizable Russian minority – some 20 percent – many of whom are skilled workers. They are now leaving the country.

President Akayez would like Kyrgyzstan to be a democratic state holding a position in central Asia similar to that of Switzerland in Europe – neutral, independent, and prosperous. The country is modernizing slowly, and trade links are growing with Turkey, Iran, and China, who are interested in joint venture projects. In the short term the economic position is uncertain. In 1991 the Russian Federation had to give Kyrgyzstan the money it needed to cover its expenses.

In Kyrgyzstan's favor it should be said that President Akayev is committed to reforming the economy, reversing collectivization, and improving land use. These policies have been praised by the United States and Western European countries. The U.S. Secretary of State, James Baker, visited Bishkek in December 1991, and later the United States was the first foreign power to send its representatives to Kyrgyzstan. Saudi Arabia has also shown that it is willing to help this Muslim country. If President Akayev can guide his country safely to democracy, Kyrgyzstan is more likely to succeed in the future than some of its neighbors in central Asia.

James Baker, former U.S. Secretary of State

FACTS AND FIGURES

Uzbekistan

Area 172,587 sq miles (447,000 sq km).

Population 20,300,000 (1990).

Population density 117 persons per sq mile (45 per sq km).

Capital Tashkent, population 2,075,000 (1989).

Other main cities Samarkand, Fergana, Bukhara.

Natural resources Natural gas, oil, gold (7th largest producer in the world), lead.

Industry Chemicals, metal working, steel making.

Agriculture Cotton, grain, tobacco, fruit, livestock.

Main minorities Russians, 8 percent (1988).

Ruler President Islam Karimov of the People's Democratic Party of Uzbekistan.

Turkmenistan

Area 188,417 sq miles (488,000 sq km).

Population 3,600,000 (1990).

Population density 18 persons per sq mile (7 per sq km).

Capital Ashkhabad, pop-

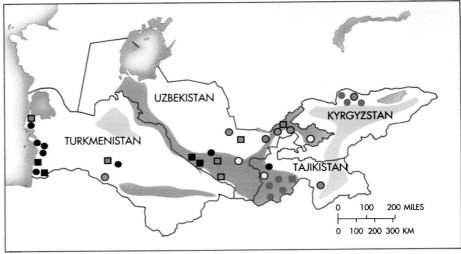

RESOURCES

- ■ Natural gas
- ● Petroleum
- ● Electricity generation
- ■ Copper
- ● Mechanical engineering
- ▫ Textiles
- ○ Gold
- ● Lead
- ▫ Chemical industry
- ▨ Irrigated land
- ▨ Livestock farming

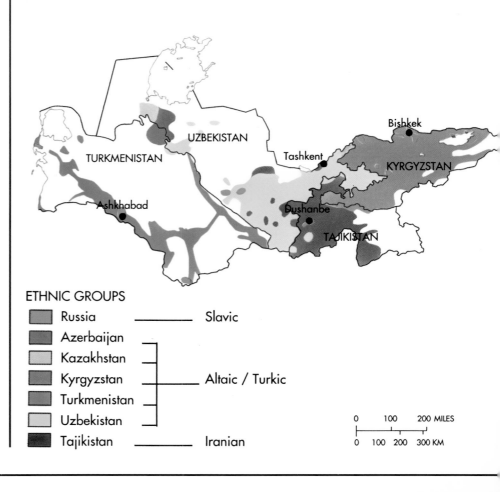

ETHNIC GROUPS

- Russia ——————— Slavic
- Azerbaijan
- Kazakhstan ┐
- Kyrgyzstan ├ Altaic / Turkic
- Turkmenistan │
- Uzbekistan ┘
- Tajikistan ——————— Iranian

ulation 400,000 (1989).
Natural resources
Natural gas (annual production, 90 billion cubic meters), oil.
Industry Metal working, electricity generation.
Agriculture Mixed farming, livestock, cotton, fisheries.
Main minorities Uzbeks and Russians, both 9 percent (1988).
Ruler President Sapar-murad Niyazov of the Democratic Party of Turkmenistan.

Tajikstan
Area 55,212 sq miles (143,000 sq km).
Population 5,250,000.
Population density 93 persons per sq mile (36 per sq km).
Capital Dushanbe, pop-

ulation 590,000 (1989).
Natural resources
Copper, lead, oil, natural gas, uranium.
Industry Metal working, hydroelectricity, textiles, aluminum.
Agriculture Cotton, grain, livestock farming.
Main minorities Uzbeks, 23 percent, Russians 7 percent (1988).
Ruler Muslim religious leader, Qadi Akbar Turadzhon-Zoda.

Kyrgyzstan
Area 76,900 sq miles (199,000 sq km).
Population 4,400,000

(1990).
Population density 56 persons per sq mile (22 per sq km).
Capital Bishkek, formerly Frunze, population 615,000 (1989).
Natural resources
Hydroelectricity, coal, silver.
Industry Metal working.
Agriculture Grain, livestock farming, sheep, goats, and horses.
Main minorities Russians 22 percent, Uzbeks 12 percent (1988).
Ruler President Askar Akayev of the Democratic Party of Kyrgyzstan.

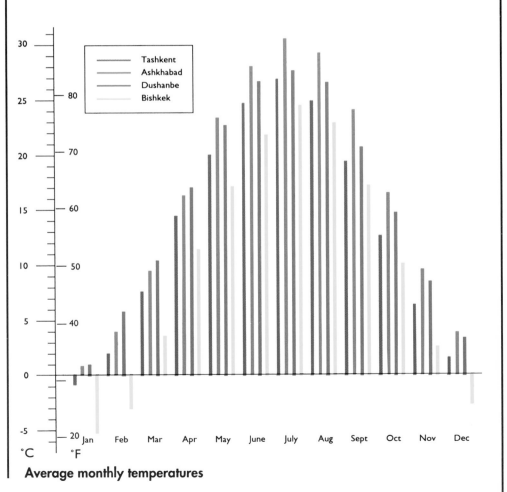

National income per head, 1988

Average monthly temperatures

CHRONOLOGY AND FAMOUS PEOPLE

40,000 B.C. Evidence of classical Neanderthal man at Teshik Tash in Himalayan Range

3000 B.C. Era of mobile pastoralists in central Asia

2000 B.C. Aryan peoples (Iranian) in central Asia. Early trade on the Silk Road

600 B.C. Establishment of the Persian Empire

334 B.C. Alexander the Great invades Asia

331 B.C. Persians defeated at Battle of Gaugamela. Persian Empire overthrown by Alexander

323 B.C. Death of Alexander the Great

247 B.C. Parthians invade present-day Turkmenistan

138 B.C. Chang Ch'ien, Chinese emissary, visits Fergana Valley for "heavenly horses"

130 B.C. Scythians invade central Asia

A. D. 632 Birth of the Prophet Muhammad

710 Samarkand captured by Arab invaders

1040 Seljuk Turks invade Transoxiana

1162 Probable birth date of Genghis Khan in Mongolia

1219 Mongols capture Bukhara and Samarkand

1227 Death of Genghis Khan

1240 Kiev sacked by the Mongols

1273 Marco Polo travels in the Pamir mountain range

1533 State of Muscovy reaches the Ural Mountains

1647 Russia expands its empire to Pacific Ocean

1717 Russian expedition to Khiva

1861 Alexander II

Joseph Stalin (1879-1953) established the communist system in the Central Asian States after the death of Lenin. His forced collectivization of agriculture damaged the economy of Central Asia.

Mikhail Gorbachev (1931-) became general secretary of the Communist Party in 1985. He introduced *perestroika* and *glasnost,* but resigned in 1992 as the Soviet Union dissolved.

abolishes serfdom in Russia

1864 Russia invades central Asia

1865 Tashkent captured by the Russians

1873 Khiva surrenders to the Russians

1880 Construction of Trans-Caspian Railroad begins

1888 Trans-Caspian Railroad completed at Tashkent

1905 Russia defeated in Russo-Japanese War

1917 February Tsar Nicholas II abdicates after

Askar Akayez (1943-) pursued a career as a physicist in Leningrad for 15 years. He was elected president of Kyrgyzstan in 1990. A reformer, he is respected both at home and abroad.

the Russian Revolution;
October The communists seize power in Petrograd
1918-21 Civil war in the Russian Empire
1924 Death of Lenin
1925 Uzbek, Tajik, and Turkmen republics established
1930 Forced collectivization of agriculture in Soviet Russia and beginning of rapid industrialization
1936 Republic of Kyrgyzia created
1937 Stalin purges the

communists in the central Asian republics
1953 Death of Stalin, succeeded by Khrushchev
1964 Fall of Khrushchev, succeeded by Brezhnev
1979 Soviet invasion of Afghanistan
1982 Death of Brezhnev
1985 Gorbachev comes to power in the Soviet Union
1986 Gorbachev launches *glasnost*
1987 Gorbachev launches *perestroika*
1988 Soviet Union with-

Akbar Turadzhon-Zoda (1943-) became influential in Tajikistan following the downfall of President Nabiev in 1992. As spiritual leader of Tajik Muslims, he plays a role similar to the late Ayatollah Khomeini in Iran.

Saparmurad Niyazov (1940-) is a hardline communist. He became head of the Communist Party of Turkmenistan in 1985, and president of the newly independent state in 1991.

draws from Afghanistan
1989 Ethnic disturbances involving Uzbeks and Meskhetians
1990 Islamic Renaissance Party founded in Ashkhabad
1991 February Riots in Tajikistan
August Attempted coup against Gorbachev
December Gorbachev resigns as Soviet Union is dissolved; creation of the C.I.S. The central Asian states gain independence
1992 May Nabiev overthrown in Tajikistan

INDEX

PHOTOCREDITS

All the pictures in this book were supplied by Novosti RIA apart from the front cover: U.S.S.R. Photo Library; pages 7 top, 23 top, 26, 27 both and 31 bottom: Frank Spooner Pictures; 12, 13, 15 & 17 top: Mary Evans Picture Library; 17 bottom: The Hulton Picture Company.